VEGGIE
BOWLS

ORATHAY SOUKSISAVANH
PHOTOGRAPHY BY AKIKO IDA

VEGGIE BOWLS

Hardie Grant

BOOKS

CONTENTS

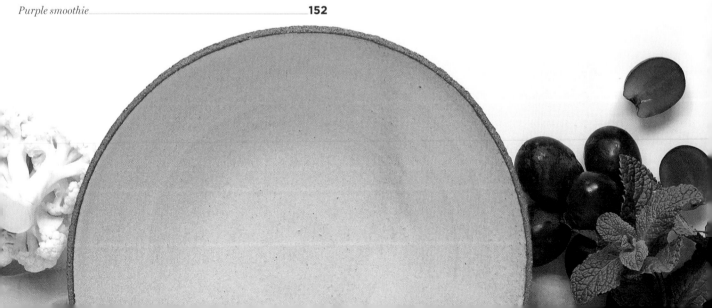

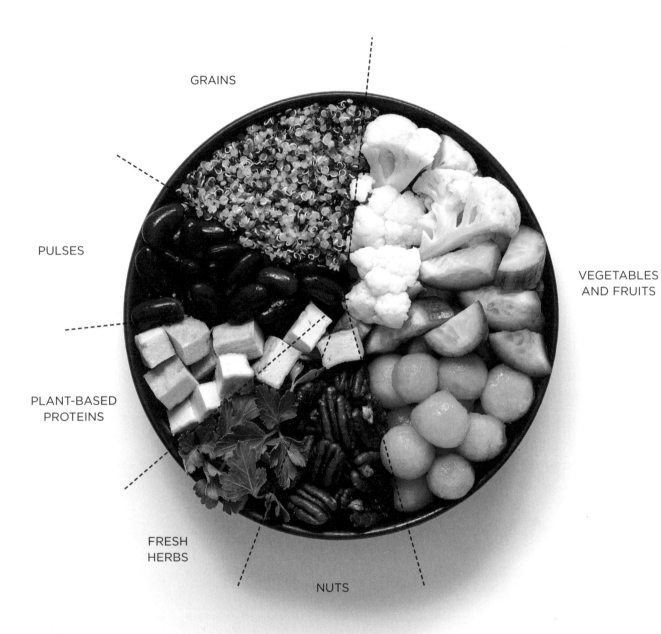

GRAINS

PULSES

VEGETABLES
AND FRUITS

PLANT-BASED
PROTEINS

FRESH
HERBS

NUTS

WHAT IS BOWL FOOD?

Bowl food is a complete meal in a bowl. It contains a mixture of small portions of several ingredients to form a balanced whole.

The ideal base ingredients are:

– a source of carbohydrates (grains, potato, sweet potato, bread, etc.)

– a source of protein (pulses, tofu, tempeh, cheese, etc.)

– plenty of vegetables.

Toppings and dressings can then be added for a delicious and indulgent final touch.

Bowl food is also about making your meal look beautiful through a harmonious combination of different textures and colours.

The idea is to create an 'edible rainbow' and get as many vitamins and nutrients as possible by mixing raw, cooked, fermented, crunchy and creamy ingredients.

Bowl food also comes in sweet versions for a healthy and tasty breakfast or snack.

Say yes to fruit and veg with these delicious sweet and savoury vegetarian recipes!

THE DIFFERENT BOWLS

1.

HOW TO MAKE A VEGGIE BOWL

Raw and/or cooked vegetables

+ **1 starchy food:** rice, grains, couscous, noodles, bread, etc.
+ **1 portion of pulses and/ or 1 dip:** hummus, tzatziki, etc.
+ **1 protein:** egg, cheese, vegetable-based protein (tofu, tempeh, seitan, etc.)
+ **1 item of fruit**
+ **toppings:** seeds, herbs, nuts, spices, etc.
+ **1 dressing**
+ **1 sauce**

2.

HOW TO MAKE A SMOOTHIE BOWL

Base

1 frozen thickener ingredient: banana, mango

+ **1 liquid:** plant-based milk, fruit juice, yoghurt or milk
+ **fruit:** frozen fruit or flavouring (cocoa/ unsweetened chocolate powder, peanut butter, matcha powder, etc.)

Optional extras

1 frozen leafy green vegetable: spinach, kale, rocket (arugula), celery leaves, etc.

1 sweetener ingredient

Toppings

Chopped fruit
Seeds
Nuts
Dried fruit
Grains
Chocolate

3.

HOW TO MAKE BIRCHER MUESLI

Base

Grain flakes: oats, rye, barley, spelt, etc.

+ **1 liquid:** plant-based milk or yoghurt or milk
+ **1 sweetener ingredient:** sugar, honey, maple syrup, agave syrup, coconut syrup, etc.
+ **Optional grated fruit:** apple, pear

Toppings

Chopped fruit
Seeds
Nuts
Dried fruit
Chocolate
Fruit coulis

UNCOOKED/COOKED EQUIVALENTS

100 g (3½ oz/½ cup) uncooked brown rice = 220 g (7¾ oz/scant 1¼ cups) cooked	*25–30 minutes in boiling water*
100 g (3½ oz) uncooked soba noodles = 235 g (8¼ oz) cooked	*3–5 minutes in boiling water*
100 g (3½ oz) dried rice noodles = 190 g (6¾ oz) cooked	*Soak for 20 minutes in cold water to rehydrate, then cook for 2–3 minutes in boiling water*
100 g (3½ oz) shelled edamame beans = 120 g (4 oz) in pods	*Follow packet instructions*
100 g (3½ oz/generous ½ cup) green lentils = 220 g (7¾ oz/scant 1¼ cups) cooked	*20–25 minutes in boiling water*
100 g (3½ oz/generous ½ cup) wholewheat couscous = 215 g (7½ oz/scant 1¼ cups) cooked	*Leave to stand for 5 minutes in the same volume of boiled water*
100 g (3½ oz/generous 1 cup) wholewheat pasta = 205 g (7¼ oz/2¼ cups) cooked	*Follow packet instructions*
100 g (3½ oz/½ cup) quinoa = 250 g (9 oz/1¼ cups) cooked	*20 minutes in boiling water*

4.

HOW TO MAKE
A CHIA PUDDING

Base

Chia seeds

+ 1 liquid: plant-based milk or milk, fruit juice, herbal tea, etc.

+ 1 sweetener ingredient: sugar, honey, maple syrup, agave syrup, coconut syrup, etc.

Toppings

Chopped fruit

Fruit coulis

Seeds

Nuts

Dried fruit

Grains

Optional flavourings

Cocoa (unsweetened chocolate) powder, matcha powder, orange blossom water, vanilla, etc.

5.

HOW TO MAKE
A SAVOURY BOWL CAKE

Base

1 grain: your choice of flaked grains

or **1 powder:** flour, polenta, buckwheat flour, etc.

+ 1 egg

Optional savoury flavourings

Cheese, tapenade, herbs, spices, etc.

Toppings

Seeds

Nuts

Herbs

Olives, etc.

Lettuce, baby leaves

Cooking time

2 minutes in the microwave at 900 W, then add 30 seconds at a time until the right texture is reached

COOKING GREEN VEGETABLES TO RETAIN SOME CRUNCH

Mangetout peas (snow peas): 1 minute in salted boiling water

Broccoli florets: 1 to 3 minutes in salted boiling water

Green beans: 5 to 8 minutes in salted boiling water depending on size and variety

PLANT-BASED PROTEINS

SEITAN

TEMPEH

FRIED TOFU

FIRM TOFU

SOYA PROTEIN
CHUNKS

PLANT-BASED
MEATBALLS

PLANT-BASED
PROTEIN PIECES

SILKEN TOFU

PULSES

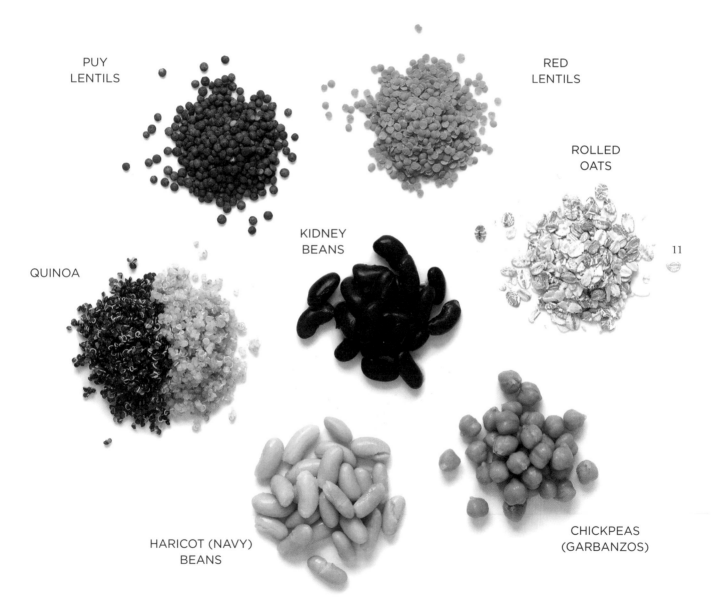

PUY LENTILS

RED LENTILS

ROLLED OATS

QUINOA

KIDNEY BEANS

11

HARICOT (NAVY) BEANS

CHICKPEAS (GARBANZOS)

STARCHY FOODS

PASTA

WHOLEWHEAT
COUSCOUS

SOBA
NOODLES

12

BROWN
RICE

RICE
NOODLES

RAMEN
NOODLES

NUTS

HAZELNUTS
(FILBERTS)

PECANS

ALMONDS

WALNUTS

PEANUTS

PISTACHIOS

PEANUT
BUTTER

13

CASHEWS

ALMOND
BUTTER

CASHEW NUT
BUTTER

SWEET & SAVOURY TOPPINGS

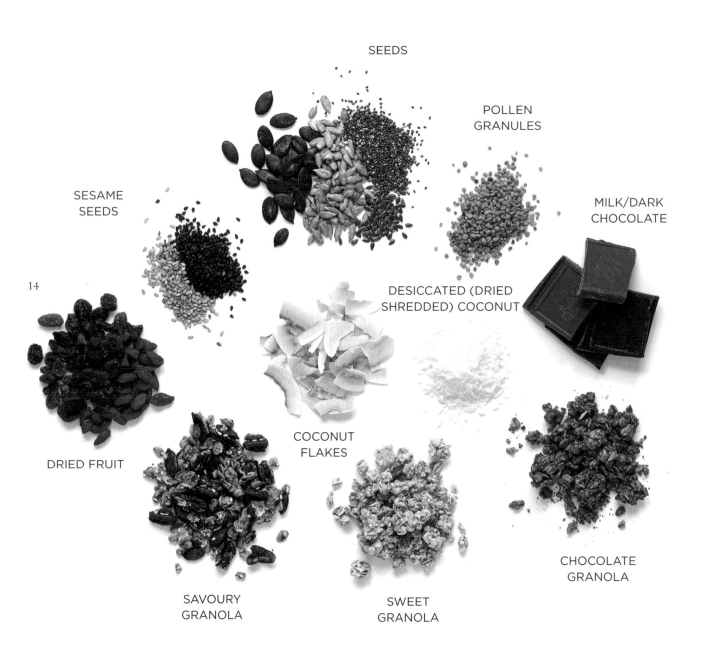

SEEDS

POLLEN
GRANULES

SESAME
SEEDS

MILK/DARK
CHOCOLATE

14

DESICCATED (DRIED
SHREDDED) COCONUT

DRIED FRUIT

COCONUT
FLAKES

CHOCOLATE
GRANOLA

SAVOURY
GRANOLA

SWEET
GRANOLA

CONDIMENTS

CHILLI

SPICES

MISO

FRESH HERBS

MUSTARD

HARISSA
PASTE

SHERRY
VINEGAR

PRESERVED
LEMON

GARLIC

SOY SAUCE

THYME,
OREGANO

GINGER

SPRING ONION

ONION,
SHALLOT

15

FAST IN 15'

Easy recipes

for delicious food in no time.

GREEK SALAD

Preparation: 15 minutes

For 1 bowl

1 little gem (bibb lettuce) or 1 cos (romaine) lettuce heart
60 g (2 oz) feta
200 g (7 oz) cherry tomatoes, halved
⅓ cucumber, cut into half rounds
¼ green (bell) pepper, thinly sliced
¼ red onion, thinly sliced

Toppings, dressing and sides
1 tablespoon sherry vinegar
2 tablespoons olive oil
60 g (2 oz) kalamata olives
dried oregano
salt and pepper
½ pitta bread, warmed in toaster

method

Break off the lettuce leaves and chop coarsely. Break the feta into pieces.
To make the dressing, whisk the vinegar and oil together and season to taste.
Arrange all the elements in separate parts of the bowl.
Add the olives and sprinkle with oregano.
Drizzle with the dressing. Serve with the pitta bread.

CAESAR SALAD

Preparation: 10 minutes
Cooking time: 7 minutes

20

For 1 bowl

1 large egg
1 small cos (romaine) lettuce heart, cut into pieces
½ avocado, sliced
80 g (2¾ oz) plant-based protein pieces
40 g (1½ oz) croutons

Topping and dressing

1 Creamy Vegan Dressing (page 178)
1 tablespoon capers
1 sprig of flat-leaf parsley, snipped (optional)

method

Cook the egg for 7 minutes until soft-boiled. Cool in cold water, then peel.
Mix the creamy dressing with the capers. Arrange all the elements in separate
parts of the bowl. Sprinkle with parsley (if using) and serve with the dressing.

ANTIPASTI

Preparation: 10 minutes
Cooking time: 5 minutes

For 2 bowls

600 g (1 lb 5 oz) defrosted grilled vegetables
4 small tomatoes, cut into wedges
4 artichoke hearts in oil, halved
80 g (2¾ oz) olives
100 g (3½ oz) rocket (arugula)

Dressing and sides

3 tablespoons balsamic vinegar
4 tablespoons olive oil
salt and pepper
4 slices of focaccia

method

Season the defrosted vegetables. Drizzle with olive oil and grill (broil) for 5 minutes. To make the dressing, whisk the vinegar and oil together and season to taste. Arrange all the elements in separate parts of each bowl. Drizzle with the dressing and serve with the focaccia. You can also add snipped basil and Parmesan shavings or mozzarella balls to this dish.

CAPRESE

Preparation: 10 minutes

For 1 bowl

250 g (9 oz) assorted tomatoes, cut into wedges
150 g (5½ oz) melon, balled or cut into cubes
handful (about 40 g/1½ oz) of rocket (arugula)
1 small burrata (120 g/4 oz)

Topping, dressing and sides
1 sprig of basil
2 tablespoons balsamic vinegar
2 tablespoons olive oil
salt and pepper
1 or 2 slices of toasted sourdough bread

method

To make the dressing, whisk the vinegar and oil together and season. Arrange the elements in separate parts of the bowl. Add whole basil leaves or tear them roughly by hand. Drizzle with the dressing and serve with the bread. You can also tear the bread into pieces and mix with the salad.

NEXT-LEVEL NOODLES

Preparation: 5 minutes
Cooking time: 9 minutes

For 1 bowl

1 tablespoon dried black mushrooms
1 pack instant noodles (flavour of your choice)
2 Chinese (napa) cabbage leaves, coarsely chopped
35 g (1¼ oz) mangetout (snow peas)

60 g (2 oz) smoked tofu, cut into thin slices
Topping
½ teaspoon black sesame seeds

method

Coarsely crush the mushrooms using the bottom of a jar.
Add the amount of water required to cook the noodles to a saucepan.
Add the mushrooms, bring to a boil and cook for 5 minutes. Add the
contents of the condiment sachet and the noodles. Cook for 2 minutes,
then add the cabbage, mangetout and tofu. Continue cooking for
1–2 minutes. Pour into a bowl. Sprinkle with the sesame seeds.

INSTANT NOODLES

Preparation: 5 minutes
Cooking time: 5 minutes

28

For 1 bowl

1 pack instant noodles (flavour of your choice)
2 closed cup mushrooms, thinly sliced
½ leek, cut into rounds

35 g (1¼ oz) spinach, stems removed
15 g (½ oz) bean sprouts
chilli powder, to taste

method

Add the amount of water needed to cook the noodles to a saucepan.
Add the contents of the condiment sachet, the noodles, mushrooms and leek.
Cook for about 3–4 minutes. When the noodles are cooked, add the spinach
and bean sprouts. Mix together and pour into a bowl. Serve with a little chilli powder.
You can also add a soft-boiled egg to this dish.

MEZZE BOWL

Preparation: 10 minutes

30

For 1 bowl

60 g (2 oz) Lebanese tabouleh from the deli counter
50 g (1¾ oz) hummus of your choice
50 g (1¾ oz) aubergine (eggplant) dip
50 g (1¾ oz) pickled vegetables (optional)
2 warmed falafels
120 g (4 oz) tomatoes, cut into wedges
   or large dice

¼ cucumber or ½ baby cucumber,
   cut into rounds
1 little gem (bibb lettuce), leaves removed

Dressing and sides

1 lemon wedge
olive oil, to drizzle
1 Lebanese-style flatbread, quartered

method

Arrange all the elements in separate parts of a large bowl or shallow dish.
Squeeze the lemon juice over the raw vegetables.
Drizzle with a little oil. You can also season the raw vegetables
with a little sea salt and freshly ground pepper.
Serve with the flatbread.

HARICOT BEANS, PEPPERS & LITTLE GEM LETTUCE

Preparation: 10 minutes

32

For 1 bowl

150 g (5½ oz) tinned haricot (navy) beans,
  drained and rinsed
150 g (5½ oz) tomatoes, cut into wedges
  or large dice
3 piquillo peppers or 1 roasted red (bell) pepper
  from a jar, cut into thin strips
2 little gems (bibb lettuce) or 1 lettuce heart,
  leaves removed

1 wedge of red onion, finely sliced
2 tablespoons olives

Topping and dressing

2 tablespoons sherry vinegar
1 tablespoon olive oil
2 sprigs of flat-leaf parsley, snipped
salt and pepper

method

To make the dressing, whisk the vinegar and oil together and season to taste.
Arrange all the elements in separate parts of a large bowl or shallow dish.
Sprinkle with parsley and serve drizzled with the dressing.
You can also add a hard-boiled egg, cut into wedges, to this dish.

MEXICAN SALAD

Preparation: 10 minutes
Cooking time: 10 minutes

34

For 1 bowl

100 g (3½ oz) tinned kidney beans, drained
  and rinsed
100 g (3½ oz) tinned sweetcorn, drained
4 slices of sweet potato, toasted 3 times
  in a toaster
1 little gem (bibb lettuce) or 1 lettuce heart,
  leaves removed
150 g (5½ oz) cherry tomatoes, halved
¼ cucumber, cut into cubes

1 small wedge of red (bell) pepper, thinly sliced
¼ or ½ avocado, thinly sliced

Toppings and dressing

2 tablespoons olive oil
juice of ½ lime
¼ red onion, finely chopped
¼ green chilli, thinly sliced (optional)
3 sprigs of coriander (cilantro) leaves
salt and pepper

method

To make the dressing, whisk the olive oil and lime juice together
and season to taste. Arrange all the elements in separate parts of a large
bowl or shallow dish. Sprinkle with the onion, chilli and coriander leaves.
Serve drizzled with the dressing. You can also cook the
sweet potato for 5 minutes under the grill (broiler).

WALDORF SALAD

Preparation: 10 minutes

36

For 1 bowl

1 small bunch of grapes
1 small cos (romaine) lettuce heart, coarsely chopped
2 celery stalks, thinly sliced
30 g (1 oz) baby spinach leaves
½ apple, cut into cubes

100 g (3½ oz) plant-based protein pieces,
 either heated or cold, as preferred

Topping and dressing
5 walnut halves, coarsely chopped
1 Creamy Vegan Dressing (page 178)

method

Halve the grapes or leave whole. Arrange all the elements in
separate parts of a large bowl or shallow dish. Sprinkle with the
walnuts. Serve with the creamy dressing. You can also add a soft-
boiled egg to this dish and replace the grapes with cranberries.

INDIAN SALAD

Preparation: 10 minutes

For 1 bowl

1 portion (150 g/5½ oz) Indian Rice (page 188), heated
60 g (2 oz) Tzatziki (page 174 or store-bought)
125 g (4½ oz) cherry tomatoes, halved
60 g (2 oz) red and/or white cabbage, finely sliced on a mandolin

Toppings and dressing

1 tablespoon raisins
25 g (¾ oz) cashews
3 sprigs of coriander (cilantro), leaves picked
juice of ½ lime
salt and pepper

method

Arrange all the elements in separate parts of a large bowl or
shallow dish. Sprinkle with the raisins, cashews and coriander
leaves. Season the raw vegetables with a squeeze of lime juice and
a little salt and freshly ground pepper. You can also add a drizzle
of olive oil and some plant-based protein pieces to this dish.

SALAD, OMELETTE, MANGO & PEANUTS

Preparation: 10 minutes
Cooking time: 5 minutes

40

For 1 bowl

2 eggs
1 teaspoon sweet soy sauce
1 tablespoon vegetable oil
2 little gems (bibb lettuce), leaves removed,
   or 1 Batavia lettuce heart
40 g (1½ oz) rocket (arugula)
¼ cucumber or 1 baby cucumber,
   cut into fine slices lengthways

¼ or ½ mango, cut into thin slices or cubes
1 small handful of sprouted seeds of your choice

Toppings and dressing

1 spring onion (scallion), thinly sliced
2 tablespoons salted roasted peanuts
3 sprigs of coriander (cilantro), leaves picked
1 Peanut and Ginger Dressing (page 177)

method

Whisk the eggs with the soy sauce. Heat the oil in a frying pan (skillet) and make two thin omelettes. Roll the omelettes and slice into thin strips. Arrange all the elements in separate parts of a large bowl or shallow dish. Sprinkle with the spring onion, peanuts and coriander leaves. Serve drizzled with the dressing. You can also add chopped coriander to the omelette and sprinkle the dish with mint.

COMTÉ, MUSTARD & PARSLEY BOWL CAKE

Preparation: 5 minutes
Cooking time: 3 minutes

42

For 1 bowl

1 egg
40 g (1½ oz/2½ tablespoon) milk
1 teaspoon baking powder
1 heaped tablespoon wholegrain mustard
2 sprigs of flat-leaf parsley, snipped
35 g (1¼ oz) Comté, grated
45 g (1½ oz) rolled oats

Toppings and dressing

1 tablespoon sherry vinegar
1 tablespoon olive oil
30 g (1 oz) lamb's lettuce
5 walnut halves
1 tablespoon dried cranberries
salt and pepper

method

In a bowl, whisk together the egg, milk, baking powder and 1 heaped teaspoon of mustard. Add the parsley, Comté and rolled oats. Mix together and cook for 2½ minutesin the microwave at 800 W. The centre of the cake should not be wet. Cook for an additional 30 seconds if necessary. To make the dressing, whisk the remaining mustard, vinegar and oil together. Season to taste with salt and pepper. Loosen the edges of the bowl cake with a spatula and turn out onto a plate. Serve with the lamb's lettuce, walnuts, cranberries and dressing.

TOMATO & OLIVE BOWL CAKE

Preparation: 10 minutes
Cooking time: 3 minutes

44

For 1 bowl

1 egg
60 g (2 oz/4 tablespoons) milk
1 teaspoon baking powder
1 tablespoon sun-dried tomato paste
45 g (1½ oz) flour
20 g (¾ oz/about 1 tablespoon) black olives, coarsely
  chopped

Toppings and dressing

1 tablespoon balsamic vinegar
1 tablespoon olive oil
2 artichoke hearts in oil, halved or quartered
30 g (1 oz) rocket (arugula)
125 g (4½ oz) cherry tomatoes, halved
salt and pepper

method

In a bowl, whisk together the egg, milk, baking powder and tomato paste. Add the flour and mix together, then add the olives. Cook for 2½ minutes in the microwave at 800 W. The centre of the cake should not be wet. Cook for an additional 30 seconds if necessary. To make the dressing, whisk the balsamic vinegar and olive oil together and season to taste. Loosen the edges of the bowl cake with a spatula and turn out onto a plate. Serve with the raw vegetables and dressing.

VEGGIE BALL BOWL

Preparation: 10 minutes

46

For 1 bowl

1 portion vegetarian meatballs of your choice, heated
1 carrot, grated
⅓ cucumber, cut into half rounds
4–5 radishes, cut into rounds
60 g (2 oz) mixed green salad

Topping and dressing
1 tablespoon mixed seeds (sunflower, flaxseed, etc.)
1 Creamy Vegan Dressing (page 178)

method

Arrange all the elements in separate parts of a large bowl or shallow dish.
Sprinkle with the seeds and serve with the creamy dressing.

HEALTH KICK

Colourful bowls containing raw food, cooked ingredients and
fruit for a balanced meal that tastes as good as it looks.

ULTRA GREEN

Preparation: 15 minutes

For 2 bowls

1 oakleaf lettuce heart or little gem (bibb lettuce)
60 g (2 oz) baby spinach leaves
120 g (4 oz) cooked peas
½ courgette (zucchini), cut into fine slices
½ green apple, cut into fine slices or cubes
½ avocado, cut into wedges or cubes
1 handful of sprouted seeds of your choice
100 g (3½ oz) white grapes, halved

Topping and dressing

1 teaspoon matcha tea
juice of ½ lemon
1 tablespoon agave or maple syrup
3 tablespoons olive oil
2 tablespoons pumpkin seeds
salt

method

To make the dressing, whisk the matcha tea, lemon juice, agave or maple syrup and olive oil together. Season to taste with salt. Arrange all the elements in separate parts of two large bowls or shallow dishes. Sprinkle with the pumpkin seeds. Serve drizzled with the dressing.

ULTRA VIOLET

Preparation: 15 minutes

For 2 bowls

250 g (9 oz) cooked black rice
80 g (2¾ oz) Beetroot and Sesame Seed Hummus
   (page 172)
½ grapefruit, cut into half rounds
1 small radicchio, leaves removed
2 heads of red chicory (endive), or white if
   unavailable, thinly sliced
8 radishes, cut into fine slices

Topping and dressing

1 tablespoon goji berries
4 tablespoons pomegranate seeds
1 teaspoon black sesame seeds
1 Mustard, Honey and Lemon Dressing (page 176)

method

Arrange all the elements in separate parts of two large bowls or
shallow dishes. Sprinkle with the goji berries and pomegranate
and black sesame seeds. Serve drizzled with the dressing.
You can also add some feta or burrata to this dish.

RAINBOW

Preparation: 20 minutes

54

For 2 bowls

1 small orange carrot, grated
1 small yellow carrot, grated
1 small purple carrot, grated
1 small red carrot, grated
3 Chinese (napa) cabbage leaves,
   thinly sliced
1 handful (about 60 g/2 oz) of red cabbage,
   finely sliced
150 g (5½ oz) seaweed salad

150 g (5½ oz) shelled and cooked edamame beans

Toppings and dressing

3 tablespoons salted roasted peanuts
3 sprigs of coriander (cilantro), leaves picked
1 Soy Sauce and Ginger Dressing (page 176)
Japanese chilli powder (optional)

method

Arrange all the elements in separate parts of two large bowls or shallow dishes. Sprinkle with the peanuts and coriander. Serve drizzled with the dressing. You can also add cubes of tofu and a little rice to this dish.

RASPBERRY, BEETROOT & TOMATO SALAD

Preparation: 15 minutes

For 2 bowls

4 tablespoons Beetroot and
Sesame Seed Hummus (page 172)
250 g (9 oz) cooked red quinoa
200 g (7 oz) cooked beetroot (beet),
    cut into cubes
250 g (9 oz) tomatoes of your choice, halved
    or quartered
125 g (4½ oz) raspberries

2 handfuls (about 80 g/2¾ oz) of mixed green salad
8 radishes, cut into rounds

Topping and dressing

2 tablespoons sherry or balsamic vinegar
3 tablespoons olive oil
2 teaspoons chia seeds
salt and pepper

method

To make the dressing, crush three of the raspberries in a bowl.
Season to taste. Add the vinegar and oil and whisk together. Arrange
all the elements in separate parts of two large bowls or shallow
dishes. Sprinkle with the chia seeds. Serve drizzled with the dressing.
You can also add chopped almonds and ricotta to this dish.

GOAT'S CHEESE SALAD WITH DARK BERRIES

Preparation: 15 minutes

58

For 2 bowls

1 oakleaf lettuce heart or little gem (bibb lettuce),
  leaves removed
80 g (2¾ oz) rocket (arugula)
150 g (5½ oz) cooked but crunchy green beans,
  cut into three
1 avocado, cut into cubes
70 g (2½ oz) Sainte-Maure or other goat's cheese log,
  cut into half rounds

100 g (3½ oz/⅔ cup) blueberries
100 g (3½ oz/⅔) blackberries, halved

Topping and dressing

2 tablespoons balsamic vinegar
3 tablespoons olive oil
50 g (1¾ oz/⅓ cup) almonds, chopped
salt and pepper

method

To make the dressing, whisk the vinegar and olive oil together.
Season to taste. Arrange all the elements in separate parts of two large
bowls or shallow dishes. Sprinkle with the almonds. Serve drizzled with the
dressing. You can also add half a finely chopped shallot to the dressing.

MIDDLE EASTERN SALAD

Preparation: 25 minutes

For 2 bowls

4 tablespoons Red Lentil Hummus (page 173)
  or other hummus of your choice
200 g (7 oz) vegetarian meatballs, heated
½ fennel bulb, finely sliced
2 small carrots, finely sliced lengthways on a mandolin
¼ red onion, diced
2 tomatoes of different colours, diced
⅓ cucumber, diced
¼ (bell) pepper of your choice, diced

6 dates, halved

Topping and dressing

½ preserved lemon, finely diced
juice of ½ lemon
3 tablespoons olive oil
1 teaspoon ras el hanout
40 g (1½ oz/1¼ cup) almonds, chopped
salt and pepper

method

To make the dressing, whisk the preserved lemon, lemon juice, oil and ras el hanout together. Season to taste. Mix all the diced vegetables together (onion, tomatoes, cucumber and pepper). Season to taste. You can also add chopped coriander to the vegetable mixture. Arrange all the elements in separate parts of two large bowls or shallow dishes. Sprinkle with the almonds. Serve drizzled with the dressing.

NEXT-LEVEL DHAL

Preparation: 20 minutes

62

For 1 bowl

300 g (10½ oz) Dhal (page 186), heated
200 g (7 oz) cooked brown rice, hot
200 g (7 oz) cherry tomatoes, halved,
   or 2 tomatoes, diced
¼ cucumber, diced
1 wedge of green (bell) pepper, diced
1 wedge of red onion, finely chopped
salt and pepper

Toppings and dressing

2 tablespoons coconut flakes, toasted
3 sprigs of coriander (cilantro), leaves picked
juice of ½ lime
salt and pepper

method

Arrange all the elements in separate parts of a large bowl or
shallow dish. Season the raw vegetables to taste. Sprinkle with the
coconut flakes and coriander. Serve drizzled with lime juice.

KOREAN SOBA NOODLES

Preparation: 20 minutes

For 2 bowls

1 Vegetable Patties recipe (page 184)
150 g (5½ oz) cooked matcha or plain soba noodles
2 small carrots, grated
150 g (5½ oz) cooked but crunchy green beans
¼ red (bell) pepper, thinly sliced
1 small wedge of red cabbage, finely sliced

2 small handfuls (40 g/1½ oz) of baby spinach leaves
2 small handfuls of sprouted seeds of your choice

Topping and dressing

2 teaspoons black sesame seeds
1 Gochujang Dressing (page 177)

method

Arrange all the elements in separate parts of two large bowls
or shallow dishes. Sprinkle with the sesame seeds and serve
drizzled with the dressing. You can replace the vegetable patties
with tofu or vegetarian meatballs if preferred.

SOBA NOODLES & GREEN VEGETABLES

Preparation: 15 minutes

For 2 bowls

250 g (9 oz) cooked matcha or plain soba noodles
200 g (7 oz) cooked but crunchy broccoli
1 baby cucumber or ⅓ cucumber,
 cut into fine slices lengthways
½ avocado, cut into wedges or cubes
2 handfuls (50 g/1¾ oz) of lamb's lettuce

150 g (5½ oz) smoked tofu, cut into cubes

Toppings and dressing

1 spring onion (scallion), thinly sliced
2 teaspoons mixed seeds (sunflower,
 flaxseed, etc.)
1 Soy Sauce and Ginger Dressing (page 176)

method

Arrange all the elements in separate parts of two large bowls or shallow dishes.
Sprinkle with the spring onion and seeds. Serve drizzled with the dressing.

NIÇOISE SALAD

Preparation: 20 minutes

For 2 bowls

125 g (4½ oz) mixed green salad
100 g (3½ oz) broad (fava) beans, peeled
6 radishes, cut into rounds
200 g (7 oz) cherry tomatoes, halved
⅓ cucumber, diced
2 celery stalks, thinly sliced
¼ red (bell) pepper, cut into strips
4 artichoke hearts, halved or quartered
2 large soft-boiled eggs, cooked for 7 minutes

Toppings and dressing

3 tablespoons sherry vinegar
4 tablespoons olive oil
80 g (2¾ oz) black or kalamata olives
1 spring onion (scallion), thinly sliced
4 sprigs of basil, leaves picked
salt and pepper

68

method

To make the dressing, whisk the vinegar and oil together and season to taste.
Arrange all the elements in separate parts of two large bowls or shallow dishes.
Sprinkle over the olives, spring onion and basil leaves. Serve drizzled with the dressing.

LENTIL, APPLE & CHICORY SALAD

Preparation: 20 minutes

For 2 bowls

200 g (7 oz) cooked dark green lentils
200 g (7 oz) celeriac (celery root), grated
2 heads of white chicory (endive),
   thinly sliced
½ apple of your choice, cut into cubes
4 radishes, finely sliced
40 g (1½ oz) lamb's lettuce
1 blood orange, peeled and cut into rounds

Toppings and dressing
juice of 1 orange
3 tablespoons balsamic vinegar
2 tablespoons walnut oil
¼ red onion or 1 shallot, finely chopped
2 tablespoons mixed seeds
   (sunflower, flaxseed, etc.)
salt and pepper

method

To make the dressing, whisk the orange juice, vinegar and oil
together and season to taste. Arrange all the elements in separate
parts of two large bowls or shallow dishes. Sprinkle with the
onion or shallot and seeds. Serve drizzled with the dressing. You
can also add smoked tofu or cubes of Comté to this dish.

GOAT'S CHEESE SALAD WITH HONEY DRESSING

Preparation: 15 minutes

For 2 bowls

1 head of white chicory (endive), leaves removed
and coarsely chopped

1 head of red chicory (endive), leaves removed
and coarsely chopped

150 g (5½ oz) celeriac (celery root), grated

1 small raw beetroot (beet), grated

30 g (1 oz) lamb's lettuce

3 kumquats, cut into thin rounds

60 g (2 oz) Sainte-Maure or other goat's cheese log,
cut into rounds

Toppings and dressing

4 tablespoons pomegranate seeds

40 g (1½ oz/generous ⅓ cup) walnut halves,
roughly chopped

1 Mustard, Honey and Lemon Dressing (page 176)

method

Arrange all the elements in separate parts of two large bowls or shallow dishes. Sprinkle with the pomegranate seeds and walnuts. Serve drizzled with the dressing. You can replace the goat's cheese with Roquefort if preferred.

CABBAGE & COUSINS

Preparation: 15 minutes

74

For 2 bowls

250 g (9 oz) cooked mixed quinoa
100 g (3½ oz) cooked cauliflower
100 g (3½ oz) cooked romanesco
100 g (3½ oz) cooked broccoli
2 Chinese (napa) cabbage leaves, finely sliced
1 small wedge of red cabbage, finely sliced
1 small apple, finely sliced or diced

Toppings and dressing

1 heaped tablespoon cashew nut butter
juice of ½ lemon
2 tablespoons olive oil
2 tablespoons dried cranberries
40 g (1½ oz/¼ cup) salted roasted cashews
salt and pepper

method

To make the dressing, mix the cashew nut butter with 2 tablespoons of hot water. Whisk in the lemon juice and olive oil. Season to taste. Arrange all the elements in separate parts of two large bowls or shallow dishes. Sprinkle with the cranberries and cashews. Serve drizzled with the dressing.

FATTOUSH

Preparation: 15 minutes
Cooking time: 6 minutes

For 2 bowls

1 Lebanese-style flatbread, cut into 6 strips
   and then into squares
1 baby cucumber, cut into rounds
8 radishes, cut into rounds
4 tomatoes, cut into wedges or cubes
¼ red onion, finely sliced
2 little gems (bibb lettuce), leaves removed
4 sprigs of parsley, leaves picked
2 sprigs of mint, leaves picked

6 small stuffed vine leaves
Topping and dressing
1 teaspoon sumac
1 tablespoon pomegranate molasses
juice of ½ lemon
olive oil
4 tablespoons pomegranate seeds
salt and pepper

method

Preheat the oven to 200°C fan (425°F/gas 7). Split the squares of bread and mix
with a good drizzle of olive oil. Season and place on a baking tray without overlapping.
Bake for 5–6 minutes. Leave to cool so the bread squares become crunchy. To make the
dressing, whisk together the sumac, molasses, lemon juice and 3 tablespoons of oil.
Season to taste. Arrange all the elements in separate parts of two large bowls
or shallow dishes. Sprinkle with the pomegranate seeds. Serve drizzled with
the dressing. You can finely chop the herbs if preferred.

BO BUN ZOODLE

Preparation: 20 minutes

For 2 bowls

1 cucumber
2 carrots
200 g (7 oz) smoked almond and sesame seed tofu
   or other tofu of your choice, cut into cubes
2 little gems (bibb lettuce) or 1 Batavia lettuce heart,
   leaves removed

Topping and dressing

3 sprigs of mint, leaves picked
3 sprigs of coriander (cilantro), leaves picked
4 tablespoons roasted peanuts
1 spring onion (scallion), thinly sliced
1 chilli, thinly sliced (optional)
1 Peanut and Ginger Dressing (page 177)

method

Spiralize the cucumber and carrots. Arrange all the elements in separate parts of two large bowls. Sprinkle with the mint, coriander, peanuts, spring onion and chilli. Serve with the peanut and ginger dressing. You can also add rice vermicelli to this dish and replace the spring onion with fried onion.

COURGETTE ZOODLE

Preparation: 20 minutes

For 2 bowls

250 g (9 oz) potatoes, steamed and
  cut into cubes
250 g (9 oz) tomatoes, cut into wedges
2 courgettes (zucchini), spiralized
60 g (2 oz) baby spinach leaves
80 g (2¾ oz) feta, crumbled into small pieces

Topping and dressing
60 g (2 oz/generous ⅓ cup) almonds, chopped
1 Yoghurt and Herb Dressing (page 179)

method

Arrange all the elements in separate parts of two large bowls
or shallow dishes. Sprinkle with the almonds. Serve with the yoghurt and herb
dressing. For a vegan version, replace the feta with olives
and blend a handful of herbs into the Creamy Vegan Dressing (page 178).

POTATOES WITH HERB DRESSING

Preparation: 15 minutes

For 2 bowls

300 g (10½ oz) small potatoes, steamed and halved
250 g (9 oz) cooked green beans, halved
  lengthways
200 g (7 oz) tomatoes of different colours,
  cut into wedges
⅓ cucumber, cut into rounds

80 g (2¾ oz) black or kalamata olives
2 handfuls (60 g/2 oz) of mixed green salad
2 hard-boiled eggs, halved or cut into wedges

Dressing

1 Yoghurt and Herb Dressing (page 179)
  or Creamy Vegan Dressing (page 178)

method

Arrange all the elements in separate parts of a large bowl or shallow dish.
Serve drizzled with the dressing. You can also add feta or Parmesan
shavings to this dish.

GOURMET
COMFORT FOOD

Cooked recipes from around the world for
delicious meals to indulge in.

BIBIMBAP

Preparation: 25 minutes

For 2 bowls

300 g (10½ oz) cooked brown rice
2 fried eggs, cooked with a drizzle of olive oil
150 g (5½ oz) cooked spinach, drained
250 g (9 oz) frozen mushrooms, pan-fried
150 g (5½ oz) frozen courgettes (zucchini),
   pan-fried
120 g (4 oz) bean sprouts, blanched
   for 10 seconds in boiling water

100 g (3½ oz) kimchi
Topping and dressing
2 teaspoons golden sesame seeds
1 Gochujang Dressing (page 177)

method

Divide the rice between the bowls or shallow dishes. Place an egg in the centre of each. Arrange all the other elements around the eggs. Sprinkle with the sesame seeds and serve drizzled with dressing. Just before eating, mix all the ingredients together.

MISO & TAHINI RAMEN

Preparation: 15 minutes
Cooking time: 5 minutes

88

For 2 bowls

1 litre (34 fl oz/4¼ cups) vegetarian dashi stock
  or vegetable stock
200 g (7 oz) tofu of your choice, cut into cubes
2 pak choi (bok choi), halved lengthways
2 closed cup mushrooms, thinly sliced
2 tablespoons tahini
2 heaped tablespoons white miso paste

250 g (9 oz) cooked ramen noodles
  or cooked fresh spaghetti

Toppings and dressing
1 small carrot, grated
2 small handfuls of sprouted leek seeds or other
  sprouted seeds of your choice
chilli oil (optional)

method

Bring the stock to a boil. Add the tofu, pak choi and mushrooms. Cook for
2 minutes. Stir the tahini and miso into the stock and mixthoroughly.
Taste and add more miso if needed. Divide the noodles between
the bowls and top with the tofu, pak choi and mushrooms
taken from the stock. Pour the hot stock over them. Add the
grated carrots, sprouted seeds and chilli oil (if using).

GREEN CURRY WITH RICE NOODLES

Preparation: 15 minutes
Cooking time: 20 minutes

For 2 bowls

40 g (1½ oz) soya protein chunks
500 ml (17 fl oz/generous 2 cups) vegetable stock
1 tablespoon Thai green curry paste
100 g (3½ oz) frozen peas
125 g (4½ oz) mangetout (snow peas)
1 small courgette (zucchini), cut into half rounds
Salt

500 ml (17 fl oz/generous 2 cups) coconut milk
300 g (10½ oz) rehydrated rice noodles
   (150 g/5½ oz dry noodles)

Topping and dressing

4 sprigs of Thai basil or coriander (cilantro)
½ lime, cut into wedges

method

Cook the soy protein in the stock with the curry paste for 15 to 18 minutes.
Season to taste with salt. Add the vegetables and cook for 2 minutes. Add the coconut
milk, bring to a boil and remove from the heat. Cook the rice noodles for 2 to 3 minutes
in a saucepan of boiling water. Drain and divide between the bowls. Pour the
curry over the top of the noodles. Add the Thai basil leaves and serve with the
lime. You can add one level teaspoon of sugar to the curry if required.

BRUNCH BOWL

Preparation: 20 minutes
Cooking time: 20–25 minutes

For 2 bowls

250 g (9 oz) closed cup mushrooms, cut into wedges
2 garlic cloves, crushed
2 tomatoes, cut in half horizontally
1 tin (about 415 g/14 oz) of baked beans, heated
2 fried eggs, cooked with a drizzle of oil
4 small frozen rösti cakes or hash browns
olive oil
salt and pepper

Topping and dressing

3 sprigs of flat-leaf parsley, snipped
3 tablespoons Savoury Granola
   (page 180, optional)
2 slices of toasted sourdough bread

method

Preheat the oven to 200°C fan (425°F/gas 7). Season the mushrooms, add half the garlic and drizzle with oil. Mix together and place on a baking tray. Put the tomatoes next to them. Season to taste, sprinkle with the remaining garlic and drizzle with oil. Place the rösti cakes on the baking tray and bake in the oven for 20 to 25 minutes, making sure they do not burn. Arrange all the elements in separate parts of two large bowls or shallow dishes. Sprinkle with the flat-leaf parsley and savoury granola. Serve with the toasted bread.

COUSCOUS BOWL

Preparation: 20 minutes
Cooking time: 25 minutes

94

For 2 bowls

3 tablespoons olive oil
1 red onion, thinly sliced
1 to 2 tomatoes, cut into pieces
1 tablespoon ras el hanout
1 garlic clove, crushed
10 g (½ oz) fresh ginger root, peeled and grated
1 litre (34 fl oz/4¼ cups) vegetable stock
2 baby yellow turnips, cut into wedges
1 large or 2 small carrots, cut into chunks
1 courgette (zucchini), cut into chunks
   and halved horizontally

30 g (1 oz/¼ cup) raisins
125 g (4½ oz) tinned chickpeas (garbanzos), drained
250 g (9 oz) cooked wholewheat couscous
salt and pepper

Toppings

5 sprigs of coriander (cilantro), leaves picked
   or snipped
harissa paste

method

Heat the oil in a saucepan. Gently fry the onion for 3 minutes.
Add the tomato, ras el hanout, garlic and ginger. Season to taste,
stir, pour in the stock and bring to a simmer. Add the turnips
and carrots and cook for 12 minutes. Add the courgette, raisins and chickpeas.
Cook for a further 5 minutes. Season to taste again if necessary. Divide the
couscous between two large bowls or shallow dishes. Drain the vegetables
and reserve the stock. Add the vegetables to the couscous and sprinkle with
the coriander. Mix the harissa paste with the stock and serve on the side.

THANKSGIVING

Preparation: 15 minutes
Resting time: 10 minutes

For 2 bowls

2–3 kale leaves, stem removed and thinly sliced
1 handful of finely sliced red cabbage
500 g (1 lb 2 oz) frozen sweet potato or butternut
   squash chunks, cooked and then mashed
5 g (¼ oz) fresh ginger root, peeled and grated
1 small pear, thinly sliced or diced

Toppings and dressing

1 tablespoon wholegrain mustard
1 tablespoon maple syrup
juice of ½ lemon
3 tablespoons walnut oil
3 tablespoons dried cranberries
4 tablespoons Savoury Granola (page 180)
   or 40 g (1½ oz/generous ⅓ cup) pecans
salt and pepper

method

To make the dressing, whisk the mustard, maple syrup, lemon juice and oil together. Season to taste. Season the kale and cabbage with salt and pepper in two different bowls. Mix the seasoning in and leave to stand for 10 minutes. Season the sweet potato mash and add the ginger. Arrange all the elements in separate parts of two large bowls or shallow dishes. Sprinkle with the cranberries and savoury granola. Drizzle with the dressing. You can also add butter or fresh cream to the sweet potato mash.

NOODLES WITH AUBERGINE & MISO

Preparation: 20 minutes
Cooking time: 25 minutes

For 2 bowls

1 aubergine (eggplant) weighing about
   300 g (10½ oz), halved lengthways
40 g (1½ oz) white miso paste
10 g (½ oz) fresh ginger root, peeled and grated
2 tablespoons mirin
1 heaped teaspoon sugar
2 bundles of cooked black rice or soba noodles
   (160 g/5½ oz dry noodles)
150 g (5½ oz) cooked green beans, halved lengthways

1 baby cucumber or ⅓ cucumber,
   cut into fine slices lengthways
160 g (5½ oz) Japanese-style tofu, cut into cubes
2 small handfuls of sprouted seeds of your choice

Toppings and dressing

juice of ½ lemon
olive oil
1 spring onion (scallion), thinly sliced
2 teaspoons black sesame seeds
Japanese chilli (optional)

method

Preheat the oven to 200°C fan (425°F/gas 7). Make slits in the flesh of the aubergine without cutting all the way through. Brush generously with olive oil. Bake for 20 minutes. Whisk together the miso, ginger, mirin and sugar. Generously coat the aubergines with the mixture. Set the rest aside.
Cook for a further 5 minutes under the grill (broiler). Add a squeeze of lemon juice and 2 tablespoons of olive oil to the remaining miso dressing. Arrange all the elements in separate parts of two large bowls or shallow dishes. Sprinkle with the spring onion and sesame seeds. Serve drizzled with the dressing and sprinkle with chilli (if using).

ROASTED CAULIFLOWER WITH SPICES & SEITAN

Preparation: 20 minutes
Cooking time: 20 minutes

For 2 bowls

400 g (14 oz) cauliflower florets
1 tablespoon ground cumin
1 tablespoon paprika
250 g (9 oz) seitan, cut into slices
1 small beetroot (beet), diced
1 small wedge of red cabbage, finely sliced
¼ red onion, finely sliced

Toppings and dressing

1 heaped tablespoon tahini
1 teaspoon fresh harissa paste
juice of ½ lemon
1 tablespoon honey
olive oil
4 tablespoons pomegranate seeds
3 sprigs of flat-leaf parsley, leaves picked
salt and pepper

method

Preheat the oven to 200°C fan (425°F/gas 7). Mix the cauliflower with the cumin, paprika and a good drizzle of olive oil. Season generously. Place on a baking tray and roast for 15 minutes. Drizzle the seitan with olive oil, season to taste and place on the baking tray. Cook for a further 5–7 minutes. To make the dressing, mix the tahini with 2 tablespoons of hot water. Add the harissa, lemon juice, honey and 2 tablespoons of olive oil. Season with salt. Arrange all the elements in separate parts of two large bowls or shallow dishes. Sprinkle with the pomegranate seeds and parsley leaves. Serve drizzled with the dressing.

ROASTED WINTER VEGETABLES

Preparation: 20 minutes
Cooking time: 35 minutes

For 2 bowls

250 g (9 oz) celeriac (celery root), cut into cubes
3 yellow beetroot (beet), cut into wedges
4 coloured carrots, cut into uniform chunks
1 onion, cut into wedges
3 large kale leaves, stem removed
100 g (3½ oz) cooked dark green lentils

olive oil
salt and pepper

Toppings and sides

2 tablespoons goji berries
3 sprigs of flat-leaf parsley, snipped
4 tablespoons hummus of your choice

method

Preheat the oven to 200°C fan (425°F/gas 7). Combine the celeriac, beetroot, carrots and onion in a large mixing bowl. Season to taste and add a generous drizzle of olive oil. Mix together and place in a roasting tin. Roast for 25 minutes. Season the kale, drizzle with olive oil and place it next to the other vegetables. Cook for a further 10 minutes. Arrange all the elements in separate parts of two large bowls or shallow dishes. Sprinkle with the goji berries and parsley. Serve with the hummus. You can also add one tablespoon of maple syrup to the vegetables.

YAKITORI

Preparation: 20 minutes
Cooking time: 10 minutes

For 2 bowls

8 courgette (zucchini) slices, approximately
  7–8 mm (¼–⅓ in) thick
125 g (4½ oz) tempeh, cut into 8 cubes
2 large closed cup mushrooms, cut into quarters
2 tablespoons vegetable oil of your choice
4 tablespoons yakitori sauce
250 g (9 oz) cooked brown rice

100 g (3½ oz) seaweed salad⅓ cucumber, finely sliced
  on a mandolin
120 g (4 oz) red and/or white cabbage, finely sliced

Dressing

1 Soy Sauce and Ginger Dressing (page 176)
Japanese chilli (optional)

method

Thread the courgette slices, tempeh and mushrooms alternately onto skewers. Heat the oil in a large frying pan (skillet) and cook the skewers for 3–4 minutes on each side. Add the yakitori sauce and caramelise for 1 minute on each side. Arrange all the other elements in separate parts of two large bowls or shallow dishes and place the skewers on top. Serve with the soy sauce and ginger dressing. Sprinkle with a little Japanese chilli (if using).

ROASTED CARROT, CLEMENTINE, AVOCADO & FENNEL

Preparation: 20 minutes
Cooking time: 30 minutes

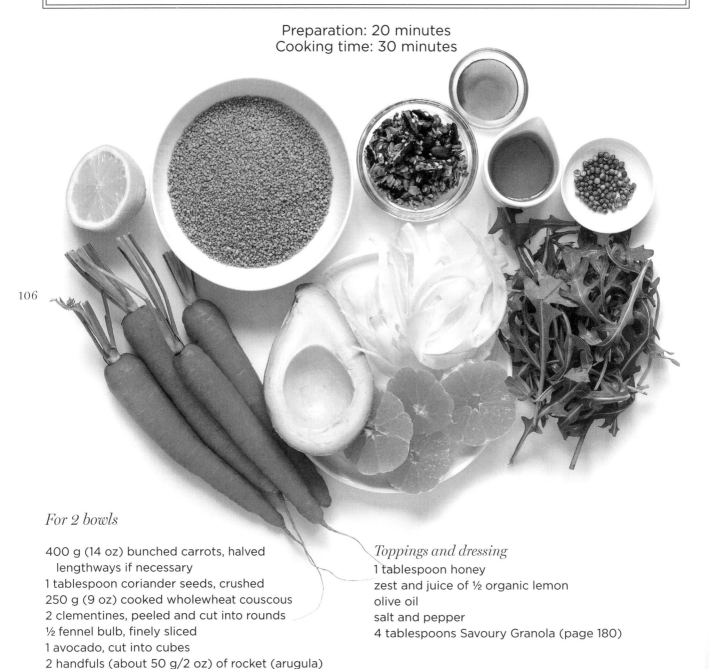

For 2 bowls

400 g (14 oz) bunched carrots, halved
    lengthways if necessary
1 tablespoon coriander seeds, crushed
250 g (9 oz) cooked wholewheat couscous
2 clementines, peeled and cut into rounds
½ fennel bulb, finely sliced
1 avocado, cut into cubes
2 handfuls (about 50 g/2 oz) of rocket (arugula)

Toppings and dressing

1 tablespoon honey
zest and juice of ½ organic lemon
olive oil
salt and pepper
4 tablespoons Savoury Granola (page 180)

method

Preheat the oven to 200°C fan (425°F/gas 7). Place the carrots in a mixing bowl and season generously. Add the coriander seeds and a good drizzle of oil. Mix together, place on a baking tray and roast for 30 minutes. To make the dressing, whisk together the honey, lemon juice and 3 tablespoons of olive oil. Season to taste. Arrange all the elements in separate parts of two large bowls or shallow dishes. Sprinkle with lemon zest and granola. Serve drizzled with the dressing.

DHAL WITH ROASTED VEGETABLES

Preparation: 10 minutes
Cooking time: 15–18 minutes

108

For 2 bowls

200 g (7 oz) cauliflower florets
200 g (7 oz) broccoli florets
1 heaped tablespoon garam masala
   or curry powder
4 tablespoons olive oil
1 small wedge of red cabbage, finely sliced

2 portions (300 g/10½ oz) Dhal (page 186), heated
salt

Topping and sides

4 sprigs of coriander (cilantro), leaves picked
2 naan breads, warmed

method

Preheat the oven to 200°C fan (425°F/gas 7). In a mixing bowl, combine the cauliflower and broccoli with the garam masala or curry powder and oil. Season generously with salt. Place on a baking tray and roast for 15–18 minutes. Arrange all the elements in separate parts of two large bowls or shallow dishes. Sprinkle with the coriander leaves. Serve with the naan bread. You can also add a squeeze of lime juice to the cabbage.

TROPICAL

Preparation: 20 minutes
Cooking time: 6 minutes

110

For 2 bowls

3 tablespoons olive oil
8 okra pods, cut into rounds
250 g (9 oz) firm tofu, cut into cubes
1 garlic clove, crushed
5 g (¼ oz) fresh ginger root, peeled and grated
2 heaped tablespoons yakitori or barbecue sauce
200 g (7 oz) cooked brown rice150 g (5½ oz) canned
kidney beans, drained and rinsed
3 cos (romaine) lettuce leaves, chopped
¼ pineapple, cut into pieces

1 small wedge of red onion, finely chopped
½ red chilli, thinly sliced
salt and pepper

Topping and dressing

4 sprigs of coriander (cilantro), snipped
juice of ½ lime

method

Heat 1 tablespoon of oil in a frying pan (skillet) and fry the okra for 2 minutes. Season to taste. Set aside. Pour the remaining oil into the same pan and brown the tofu for 2 minutes. Add the garlic, ginger and sauce. Stir and cook for a further 2 minutes. Mix the rice and beans together. Arrange all the elements in separate parts of two large bowls or shallow dishes. Sprinkle with the coriander. Add a squeeze of lime juice to the lettuce leaves.

PESTO

Preparation: 20 minutes

For 2 bowls

300 g (10½ oz) short pasta, cooked al dente
4 tablespoons pesto
150 g (5½ oz) cooked but crunchy green beans,
    cut in half or third lengths
½ small courgette (zucchini), finely sliced

40 g (1½ oz) rocket (arugula)
200 g (7 oz) cherry tomatoes, halved
salt and pepper

Topping

30 g (1 oz) Parmesan, cut into shavings

method

Toss the hot pasta with the pesto. Dilute with a little of the pasta cooking water if necessary. Arrange all the elements in separate parts of two large bowls or shallow dishes. Season the vegetables to taste. Add the Parmesan shavings. You can also add a drizzle of olive oil and a splash of balsamic vinegar to the vegetables.

SABICH

Preparation: 15 minutes
Cooking time: 5 minutes

114

For 2 bowls

150 g (5½ oz) aubergine (eggplant),
    cut into 5 mm (¼ in) slices
100 g (3½ oz) plain chickpeas (garbanzos) or Spiced
    Chickpeas (page 182)
80 g (2¾ oz) Beetroot and Sesame Seed Hummus
    (page 172) or other hummus of your choice
2–3 hard-boiled eggs, halved or quartered
200 g (7 oz) cherry tomatoes, halved
1 baby cucumber, cut into rounds
1 small wedge (about 80 g/2¾ oz) of red cabbage,
    finely sliced

Toppings, dressing and sides

1 small garlic clove, crushed
juice of ½ lemon
olive oil
¼ red onion, finely sliced
4 tablespoons pomegranate seeds
4 sprigs of flat-leaf parsley, leaves picked
2 sprigs of mint, leaves picked
salt and pepper
1 large pitta bread, warmed and cut in half

method

Preheat the oven grill (broiler). Season the aubergine to taste, add a good drizzle of olive oil, mix together and place on a baking tray. Grill for 5 minutes. To make the dressing, whisk together the garlic, lemon juice and 3 tablespoons of olive oil. Season again, as required. Arrange all the elements in separate parts of two large bowls or shallow dishes. Sprinkle with the onion, pomegranate seeds and herbs. Serve drizzled with the dressing and the pitta bread on the side.

BURRITO

Preparation: 15 minutes
Cooking time: 8–10 minutes

116

For 2 bowls

olive oil
200 g (7 oz) mixed (bell) peppers, cut into strips
½ red onion, thinly sliced
1 heaped teaspoon ground cumin
1 heaped teaspoon paprika
100 g (3½ oz) Guacamole (page 175)
150 g (5½ oz) cooked brown rice
150 g (5½ oz) Mexican flavour plant-based protein
pieces, heated

120 g (4 oz) tinned kidney beans, drained and rinsed
120 g (4 oz) tinned sweetcorn, drained
3 cos (romaine) lettuce leaves, chopped
salt and pepper

Topping and dressing

4 sprigs of coriander (cilantro), leaves picked
juice of ½ lime

method

Heat a good drizzle of olive oil in a frying pan (skillet) and brown the peppers, onion and spices for 8–10 minutes over a medium heat. Season to taste. Arrange all the elements in separate parts of two large bowls or shallow dishes. Sprinkle with the coriander. Serve with a squeeze of lime juice. You can also serve this dish with tortilla wraps.

WINTER COBB SALAD

Preparation: 15 minutes
Cooking time: 15 minutes

118

For 2 bowls

vegetable oil
250 g (9 oz) sweet potato, cut into cubes
1 small radicchio, leaves removed and
　coarsely chopped
60 g (2 oz) baby spinach leaves
1 avocado, cut into cubes
½ cooked beetroot (beet), cut into cubes
100 g (3½ oz) grapes, halved

80 g (3¾ oz) Roquefort
salt and pepper

Dressing

1 Mustard, Honey and Lemon Dressing (page 176)
　replacing the lemon with 2 tablespoons
　wine vinegar

method

Heat a drizzle of oil in a pan and cook the sweet potato for 15 minutes
over a medium heat. Season to taste. Arrange all the elements in separate parts
of two large bowls or shallow dishes. Serve drizzled with the dressing. You can also add
1 hard-boiled egg to this dish and replace the honey in the dressing with maple syrup.

NOODLES WITH PEANUT DRESSING

Preparation: 20 minutes
Cooking time: 5 minutes

For 2 bowls

3 eggs
1 tablespoon sweet soy sauce
1 tablespoon vegetable oil
200 g (7 oz) fresh cooked spaghetti
1 carrot, grated
100 g (3½ oz) red cabbage, finely sliced

70 g (2¼ oz) bean sprouts, blanched for
  10 seconds
⅓ cucumber, sliced into thin shreds

Toppings and dressing

1 spring onion (scallion), thinly sliced
2 teaspoons golden sesame seeds
1 Peanut and Ginger Dressing (page 177)

method

Whisk the eggs with the soy sauce. Heat the oil in a frying pan (skillet)
and make two thin omelettes. Roll and slice into thin strips. Arrange all the
elements in separate parts of two large bowls or shallow dishes. Sprinkle with
the spring onion and sesame seeds. Serve drizzled with the dressing.

100% FRUIT & VEG

For a shot of delicious vitamins.

GREMOLATA

Preparation: 20 minutes

124

For 2 bowls

500 g (1 lb 2 oz) mashed celeriac (celery root), heated
1 small apple, thinly sliced or cut into cubes
2 small kale leaves, stem removed
2 heads of chicory (endive), thinly sliced: 1 white
   and 1 red
1 small beetroot (beet), diced

Topping and dressing

1 garlic clove, chopped
5 sprigs of flat-leaf parsley, chopped
zest and juice of 1 organic lemon
5 tablespoons olive oil
60 g (2 oz/generous ½ cup) hazelnuts (filberts),
   toasted and chopped
salt and pepper

method

To make the dressing, whisk together the garlic, parsley, lemon zest and oil. Add a squeeze of lemon juice. Season to taste. Arrange all the elements in separate parts of two large bowls or shallow dishes. Sprinkle with the hazelnuts. Serve drizzled with the dressing. You can also add cream to the celeriac mash and sweeten the dressing with 1 teaspoon of honey.

ROASTED SUMMER VEGETABLES

Preparation: 20 minutes
Cooking time: 20 minutes

126

For 2 bowls

1 small aubergine (eggplant), cut into quarter rounds
   1 cm (½ in) wide
2 small courgettes (zucchini), cut into half rounds
   1 cm (½ in) wide
1 (bell) pepper of your choice, thinly sliced
1 onion, cut into wedges
2 sets of cherry tomatoes on the vine

2 handfuls (about 60 g/2 oz) of mixed green salad
olive oil
salt and pepper

Topping and dressing
2 tablespoons balsamic vinegar
1 sprig of oregano or 3 sprigs of thyme or basil,
   snipped

method

Preheat the oven to 200°C fan (425°F/gas 7). In a mixing bowl, prepare each vegetable separately by seasoning, adding a generous drizzle of olive oil and giving a good stir. Place the different vegetables side by side on a baking tray. Roast for 20 minutes. Leave to cool. Arrange all the elements in separate parts of two large bowls or shallow dishes. Add a splash of balsamic vinegar to the mixed green salad. Sprinkle a few oregano, thyme or basil leaves over the vegetables. You can also add Parmesan shavings or mozzarella to this dish.

VITAMIN KICK

Preparation: 20 minutes

128

For 2 bowls

½ fennel bulb, finely sliced on a mandolin
½ kohlrabi, finely sliced on a mandolin
1 small wedge of Savoy cabbage, finely sliced
½ Chioggia beetroot (beet), finely sliced
  on a mandolin
½ yellow beetroot (beet), finely sliced
6 radishes, finely sliced
2 kiwi fruit, peeled and cut into rounds
2 blood oranges, peeled and cut into rounds

Toppings and dressing
1 tablespoon honey
juice of ½ lemon
3 tablespoons olive oil
salt and pepper
2 teaspoons pollen granules
2 teaspoons sunflower seeds

method

To make the dressing, whisk together the honey, lemon juice and
olive oil. Season to taste. Arrange all the elements in separate
parts of two large bowls or shallow dishes. Sprinkle with the pollen
granules and sunflower seeds. Serve drizzled with the dressing.
You can also add chopped flat-leaf parsley to this dish.

ROASTED VEGETABLES WITH MAPLE SYRUP

Preparation: 20 minutes
Cooking time: 30 minutes

For 2 bowls

220 g (7¾ oz) parsnips, cut into large cubes
220 g (7¾ oz) sweet potato, cut into half rounds
220 g (7¾ oz) potimarron squash, cut into small
  wedges or cubes
220 g (7¾ oz) beetroot (beet), cut into small wedges
  or cubes
4 teaspoons maple syrup
8 tablespoons olive oil

4 sprigs of thyme
4 garlic cloves, unpeeled
60 g (2 oz) lamb's lettuce
salt and pepper

Toppings

zest of 1 organic lemon
40 g (1½ oz/generous ⅓ cup) pecans

method

Preheat the oven to 200°C fan (425°F/gas 7). In a mixing bowl, prepare each vegetable separately by mixing with 1 teaspoon of maple syrup, 2 tablespoons of oil and 1 sprig of thyme. Season generously. Place the vegetables side by side on a baking tray and add the unpeeled garlic. Roast for 30 minutes, stirring occasionally. Arrange all the elements in separate parts of two large bowls or shallow dishes. Zest the lemon over the vegetables and sprinkle with pecans. You can also add a squeeze of lemon juice to the lamb's lettuce.

SEA BREEZE SALAD

Preparation: 15 minutes
Marinade: 15 minutes

132

For 2 bowls

25 g (¾ oz) dried wakame (sea spaghetti), soaked
in water for about 20 minutes (until supple),
drained and roughly chopped

1 carrot, grated

125 g (4½ oz) mangetout (snow peas), cooked to
retain some crunch and cut in half

1 baby cucumber or ⅓ cucumber, cut into
fine strips lengthways

2 handfuls (about 60 g/2 oz) of mixed green salad

Toppings and dressing

1 Soy Sauce and Ginger Dressing (page 176)

4 tablespoons salted roasted peanuts

2 teaspoons sesame seeds, toasted

4 sprigs of coriander (cilantro)

method

Marinate the sea spaghetti for 15 minutes in half the dressing.
Arrange all the elements in separate parts of two large bowls
or shallow dishes. Sprinkle with the peanuts, sesame seeds and
coriander. Serve drizzled with the remaining dressing.
You can also add 1 crushed garlic clove to the half
of the dressing used as a marinade.

SEAWEED CEVICHE

Preparation: 20 minutes

134

For 2 bowls

3 sprigs of coriander (cilantro), snipped
100 g (3½ oz) mixed fresh seaweed (nori, dulse, sea lettuce), washed to remove salt, drained and chopped
2 tomatoes, diced
4 hearts of palm, diced
3 wide strips of differently coloured (bell) peppers, diced
⅓ cucumber, diced

1 small avocado, diced
¼ red onion, finely chopped
80 g (2¾ oz/½ cup) black olives, chopped

Dressing

1 teaspoon garlic powder
    or 1 small garlic clove, crushed
juice of 1 small lime
4 tablespoons olive oil
salt and pepper

method

To make the dressing, whisk together the garlic, lime juice and olive oil
and season to taste. Mix the coriander into the seaweed. Arrange all the
elements in separate parts of two large bowls or shallow dishes. Serve
drizzled with the dressing. Just before eating, mix everything together.
You can replace the fresh seaweed with seaweed tartare. In this case,
reduce the amount of dressing as the tartare is already seasoned.

CAULIFLOWER RICE

Preparation: 20 minutes

136

For 2 bowls

250 g (9 oz) raw cauliflower, grated
1 radicchio lettuce heart, leaves removed
1 small avocado, cut into slices or cubes
2 carrots, grated
1 small yellow beetroot (beet), cut into fine rounds
½ pear, finely sliced or diced
1 blood orange, peeled and cut into rounds

Toppings and dressing

1 heaped tablespoon cashew nut butter
juice of ½ orange
juice of ½ lime
2 tablespoons olive oil
1 small garlic clove, crushed
2 teaspoons pollen granules
2 teaspoons mixed seeds
  (sunflower, flaxseed, poppy seed, etc.)
salt and pepper

method

To make the dressing, mix the cashew nut butter with 2 tablespoons of hot water. Add the orange juice, lime juice, oil and garlic. Season to taste. Arrange all the elements in separate parts of two large bowls or shallow dishes. Sprinkle with the pollen and seeds. Serve drizzled with the dressing.

NABE

Preparation: 15 minutes
Cooking time: 12 minutes

138

For 2 bowls

1 small daikon radish (about 250 g/9 oz), cut into
   half rounds
1 litre (34 fl oz/4¼ cups) vegetarian dashi stock
5 g (¼ oz) fresh ginger root, peeled and grated
8 small fresh shiitake mushrooms, or 4 large
   cut into quarters
1 leek, white part only cut into angled rounds

4–6 Chinese (napa) cabbage leaves, chopped150 g
(5½ oz) firm tofu, cut into cubes
2 tablespoons dried wakame seaweed (sea spaghetti)
2 tablespoons white miso paste

Topping
2 teaspoons golden sesame seeds

method

Simmer the daikon radish for 8 minutes in the dashi stock. Add the ginger, shiitake mushrooms, leek, cabbage, tofu and wakame seaweed. Cook for a further for 3–4 minutes. Remove from the heat and add the miso paste. Mix well. Taste and add a little more miso if needed. Arrange all the elements in separate parts of two large bowls. Sprinkle with the sesame seeds. You can also accompany the soup with a small bowl of rice.

SUMMER SALAD

Preparation: 15 minutes

140

For 2 bowls

2 little gems (bibb lettuce) or 1 lettuce heart,
  leaves removed
2 handfuls (about 60 g/2 oz) of rocket (arugula)
½ baby cucumber, cut into half rounds
125 g (4½ oz) mozzarella pearls
300 g (10½ oz) melon, balled or cut into cubes
200 g (7 oz) strawberries, halved

Topping and dressing
2 tablespoons balsamic vinegar
3 tablespoons olive oil
3 sprigs of mint, snipped
salt and pepper

method

To make the dressing, whisk the vinegar and oil together and season to taste.
Arrange all the elements in separate parts of two large bowls or shallow
dishes. Sprinkle with mint and serve drizzled with the dressing. You can also
replace the strawberries with watermelon and the mozzarella with feta.

SHADES OF GREEN

Preparation: 20 minutes

For 2 bowls

½ kohlrabi, grated
1 small wedge of Savoy cabbage, finely sliced
⅓ cucumber, cut into rounds
2 little gems (bibb lettuce) or 1 lettuce heart,
  leaves removed
60 g (2 oz) baby spinach leaves

100 g (3½ oz) white grapes, halved
1 avocado, cut into cubes

Topping and dressing

3 tablespoons shelled pistachios, chopped
1 Yoghurt and Herb Dressing (page 179)

method

Arrange all the elements in separate parts of two large bowls
or shallow dishes. Sprinkle with the pistachios. Serve drizzled
with the dressing. For a vegan version, blend a handful of
herbs into the creamy vegan dressing (page 178).

SWEET TREATS

To start the day, finish a meal or treat
yourself without feeling guilty.

EXOTIC SMOOTHIE

Preparation: 15 minutes

146

For 2 bowls

200 ml (7 fl oz/scant 1 cup) coconut milk
80 g (2¾ oz) banana, cut into pieces
 and frozen the night before
200 g (7 oz) frozen mango
80 g (2¾ oz) frozen pineapple

Toppings

¼ pineapple, cut into cubes
½ mango, cut into fine slices
1 kiwi fruit, cut into rounds
pulp of 2 passion fruits
2 teaspoons desiccated coconut

method

Pour the coconut milk into a blender. Add the frozen fruit. Blend to
a creamy consistency. Add a splash more coconut milk if needed.
Pour into two bowls. Decorate with the fruit toppings and sprinkle
with the coconut. Serve immediately. You can also sweeten this
dish with a syrup of your choice: maple, agave, coconut, etc.

IN THE PINK

Preparation: 15 minutes

148

For 2 bowls

200 ml (7 fl oz/scant 1 cup) almond milk
100 g (3½ oz) frozen strawberries,
   or if unfrozen, halved and frozen the night before
80 g (2¾ oz) banana, cut into pieces
   and frozen the night before
150 g (5½ oz) frozen raspberries

Toppings

8 strawberries, halved
100 g (3½ oz) raspberries, halved
2 tablespoons pomegranate seeds
2 tablespoons almonds, chopped
2 small tablespoons goji berries

method

Pour the almond milk into a blender. Add the frozen fruit. Blend to
a creamy consistency. Add a splash more almond milk if needed.
Pour into two bowls. Decorate with the fruit toppings and almonds.
Serve immediately. You can also sprinkle this dish with chia
seeds and sweeten it with honey or maple or agave syrup.

GREEN SMOOTHIE

Preparation: 15 minutes

150

For 2 bowls

150 ml (5 fl oz/scant ⅔ cup) plant-based milk of your
    choice or apple juice
juice of ½ lime
2 tablespoons maple syrup
1 kiwi fruit, cut into pieces
80 g (2¾ oz) kale leaves, stem removed,
    or spinach leaves, frozen the night before
200 g (7 oz) pears, cut into pieces
    and frozen the night before

80 g (2¾ oz) banana, cut into pieces
    and frozen the night before
Toppings
½ green kiwi fruit, cut into half rounds
½ yellow kiwi fruit, cut into half rounds
1 clementine, cut into rounds
½ pear, thinly sliced
2 tablespoons mixed seeds
    (pollen, sunflower, flaxseed, etc.)

method

Pour the plant-based milk or apple juice into a blender. Add the lime juice,
maple syrup, kiwi fruit, kale and then all the frozen fruit. Blend to a creamy
consistency. Add a splash more liquid if needed. Pour into two bowls.
Decorate with the fruit toppings and seeds. Serve immediately.

PURPLE SMOOTHIE

Preparation: 15 minutes

For 2 bowls

100 ml (3½ fl oz/scant ½ cup) plant-based milk or milk
125 g (4½ oz) plain plant-based yoghurt or plain yoghurt
80 g (2¾ oz) banana, cut into pieces and
  frozen the night before
200 g (7 oz) frozen blueberries

Toppings

125 g (4½ oz) mixed blackberries and blueberries
2 tablespoons pomegranate seeds
2 tablespoons pistachios, chopped
2 tablespoons coconut flakes, toasted

method

Pour the plant-based milk or milk and yoghurt into a blender. Add the frozen banana and blueberries. Blend to a creamy consistency. Add a splash more liquid if needed. Sweeten with honey if required. Pour into two bowls. Decorate with the toppings. Serve immediately.

COCOA & PEANUT SMOOTHIE

Preparation: 15 minutes

154

For 2 bowls

180 g (6¼ oz) dairy-free coconut yoghurt
200 g (7 oz) banana, cut into pieces
   and frozen the night before
10 g (½ oz) unsweetened cocoa powder

Toppings

1 banana, cut into rounds
60 g (2 oz) granola of your choice
20 g (¾ oz) dark chocolate, chopped
20 g (¾ oz) milk chocolate, chopped
2 tablespoons salted roasted peanuts
2 tablespoons peanut butter

method

Pour the coconut yoghurt into a blender. Add the frozen
banana pieces and cocoa powder. Blend to a creamy consistency.
Pour into two bowls. Decorate with the toppings. Serve immediately.

CHOCOLATE CHIA PUDDING WITH DARK BERRIES

Preparation: 10 minutes
Cooking time: 2 minutes
Resting time: overnight

For 2 bowls

250 ml (8 fl oz/1 cup) oat milk
30 g (1 oz) unrefined sugar
10 g (½ oz) unsweetened cocoa powder
30 g (1 oz) chia seeds

Toppings
150 g (5½ oz) dairy-free vanilla yoghurt
80 g (2¾ oz) granola of your choice
80 g (2¾ oz) mixed blueberries and blackberries,
   halved
50 g (2 oz) dark chocolate, chopped

method

The night before, whisk the oat milk with the sugar and cocoa powder.
Bring to a boil. Pour into a jar containing the chia seeds. Mix together.
Allow to cool before refrigerating. The next day, stir the chia mix
and pour onto one side of each bowl. Add the dairy-free yoghurt to
the other side. Decorate with the toppings. Serve immediately.

MATCHA CHIA PUDDING WITH BERRIES

Preparation: 10 minutes
Cooking time: 2 minutes
Resting time: overnight

For 2 bowls

250 ml (8 fl oz/1 cup) soya milk or other
  plant-based milk
30 g (1 oz) unrefined sugar
1 tablespoon matcha powder
30 g (1 oz) chia seeds

Toppings

200 g (7 oz) raspberry coulis
200 g (7 oz) mixed fresh berries: strawberry,
  raspberry, blueberry, blackberry, halved if preferred
2 tablespoons pistachios, chopped
1 sprig of mint, snipped

method

The night before, heat the plant-based milk and sugar for 2 minutes.
Add the matcha powder and whisk. Pour into a jar containing
the chia seeds. Mix together. Allow to cool before refrigerating.
The next day, stir the chia mix and pour it onto one side of each
bowl. Add the coulis to the other side. Decorate with the fruit
toppings. Add the pistachios and mint. Serve immediately.

ALMOND CHIA PUDDING WITH APPLE & GRANOLA

Preparation: 10 minutes
Cooking time: 2 minutes
Resting time: overnight

For 2 bowls

250 ml (8 fl oz/1 cup) almond milk or other
   plant-based milk
30 g (1 oz) unrefined sugar
30 g (1 oz) chia seeds

Toppings

1 apple, diced
80 g (2¾ oz) granola of your choice
30 g (1 oz) cranberries
2 tablespoons mixed seeds
   (pumpkin, sunflower, pollen, etc.)
1 teaspoon cinnamon
2 tablespoons honey

method

The night before, heat the plant-based milk and sugar for 2 minutes. Pour into a jar containing the chia seeds. Mix together. Allow to cool before refrigerating. The next day, stir the chia mix and pour it into two bowls. Decorate with the toppings. Sprinkle with the cinnamon and drizzle with honey. Serve immediately.

PEAR, BANANA & CHOCOLATE BIRCHER

Preparation: 10 minutes
Resting time: overnight

162

For 2 bowls

250 ml (8 fl oz/1 cup) coconut milk or other
   plant-based milk
1 heaped tablespoon unrefined sugar
   or 25 g (¾ oz) maple syrup
60 g (2 oz) mixed grain flakes or rolled oats
1 organic pear, grated

Toppings

2 tablespoons hazelnut butter
1 banana, cut into rounds
2 tablespoons hazelnuts, toasted and chopped
30 g (1 oz) dark chocolate, chopped

method

The night before, mix the plant-based milk and sugar or maple syrup together. Add the grain flakes or rolled oats and grated pear. Mix together and chill. The next day, stir the Bircher and pour into two bowls. Dot with the hazelnut butter and decorate with the toppings. Serve immediately.

EXOTIC BIRCHER

Preparation: 10 minutes
Resting time: overnight

164

For 2 bowls

250 ml (8 fl oz/1 cup) coconut milk or
    other plant-based milk
1 heaped tablespoon unrefined sugar
    or 25 g (¾ oz) maple syrup
60 g (2 oz) mixed grain flakes
    or rolled oats

Toppings
100 g (3½ oz) exotic fruit coulis
    (mango, passion fruit, pineapple, etc.)
¼ mango, cut into cubes
1 wedge of pineapple, cut into cubes
½ banana, cut into rounds
80 g (2¾ oz) raspberries, halved
2 tablespoons pecans or Brazil nuts, chopped

method

The night before, mix the plant-based milk and sugar or maple
syrup together. Add the grain flakes. Mix together and chill. The
next day, stir the Bircher and pour into two bowls. Decorate with the
toppings and drizzle with the coulis. You can also add a little organic
lime zest to this dish or replace the coulis with agave syrup.

RED BERRY, POMEGRANATE & PECAN BIRCHER

Preparation: 10 minutes
Resting time: overnight

For 2 bowls

250 ml (8 fl oz/1 cup) almond milk or coconut milk
1 heaped tablespoon unrefined sugar
  or 25 g (¾ oz) maple syrup
60 g (2 oz) mixed grain flakes or rolled oats

Toppings

150 g (5½ oz) red berries, halved:
  strawberries, raspberries
3 tablespoons pomegranate seeds
2 tablespoons pecans or almonds, chopped
2 tablespoons honey
zest of 1 organic lime

method

The night before, mix the almond or coconut milk and sugar or maple syrup together. Add the grain flakes. Mix together and chill. The next day, stir the Bircher and pour into two bowls. Decorate with the toppings and drizzle with honey. Sprinkle with a little lime zest. You can also add a squeeze of lime juice to this dish.

BLUEBERRY, ALMOND & COCONUT BIRCHER

Preparation: 10 minutes
Resting time: overnight

168

For 2 bowls

250 ml (8 fl oz/1 cup) almond milk or other
  plant-based milk
1 heaped tablespoon unrefined sugar
  or 25 g (¾ oz) maple syrup
60 g (2 oz) mixed grain flakes
  or rolled oats
1 small organic apple, grated

Toppings
2 tablespoons almond butter
½ organic apple, grated
80 g (2¾ oz) blueberries, halved if preferred
30 g (1 oz/¼ cup) almonds, chopped
2 tablespoons coconut flakes, toasted

method

The night before, mix the plant-based milk and sugar or maple syrup together. Add the grain flakes and grated apple. Mix together and chill. The next day, stir the Bircher and pour into two bowls. Dot with the almond butter and decorate with the toppings. Serve immediately.

BASICS

BEETROOT & SESAME SEED HUMMUS

Preparation: 5 minutes

For 1 large bowl

240 g (8½ oz) tinned chickpeas (garbanzos), drained
200 g (7 oz) beetroot (beet), cooked and cut
   into pieces
1 tablespoon tahini

1 garlic clove
juice of ½ lemon
2 tablespoons toasted sesame oil
salt and pepper

method

Place all the ingredients in a blender apart from the
sesame oil. Blitz to a smooth paste. Season to taste, add the oil and mix
together. Check the seasoning and adjust if necessary. Store the hummus
in a jar or airtight container. It will keep for 4–5 days in the refrigerator.

RED LENTIL HUMMUS

Preparation: 5 minutes
Cooking time: 15 minutes

For 1 large bowl

100 g (3½ oz) carrots, cut into pieces
140 g (5 oz/generous ½ cup) red lentils
1 tablespoon tahini

1 teaspoon ground cumin
1 garlic clove
1 teaspoon turmeric
salt and pepper

method

Cook the carrot for 5 minutes in salted water. Add the lentils and cook for a further 10 minutes. Drain. Blitz all the ingredients in a blender. Season to taste and mix together. Taste and adjust the seasoning with a little lemon juice if necessary. Store the hummus in a jar or airtight container. It will keep for 4–5 days in the refrigerator. Add 2 or 3 tablespoons of olive oil when blending for a smoother hummus.

TZATZIKI

Preparation: 10 minutes
Resting time: 15 minutes

For 1 large bowl

1 large cucumber, cut into fine slices
200 g (7 oz) Greek yoghurt, drained
1 large garlic clove, crushed
2 sprigs of mint, chopped

2 sprigs of dill, chopped
1 tablespoon olive oil
salt and pepper

method

Season the cucumber generously with salt. Leave to drain for 15 minutes
in a colander. Then squeeze small handfuls of the cucumber between your
hands to remove any excess water. Mix with the rest of the ingredients,
then add the olive oil. Season with pepper, taste and add salt if necessary.

GUACAMOLE

Preparation: 10 minutes

For 1 large bowl

2 very ripe large avocados
1 small tomato, deseeded and diced
½ small red onion, finely chopped
juice of 1 lime

6 sprigs of coriander (cilantro), snipped
½ green chilli, deseeded and diced
salt and pepper

method

Mash the avocado flesh with a fork in a bowl. Add the remaining ingredients.
Season to taste. Taste and adjust the seasoning if necessary.
Guacamole is best eaten the same day.

MUSTARD, HONEY & LEMON DRESSING

Preparation: 5 minutes

SOY SAUCE & GINGER DRESSING

Preparation: 5 minutes

176

For 2 bowls

3 tablespoons sweet soy sauce
juice of ½ lemon
2 tablespoons olive oil
10 g (½ oz) fresh ginger root, peeled and grated
½ teaspoon Espelette pepper

For 2 bowls

1 tablespoon wholegrain mustard
juice of ½ lemon
1 tablespoon honey
3 tablespoons olive oil
salt and pepper

method

Whisk all the ingredients
together. Season to taste.

method

Whisk all the ingredients
together. You can also
add half a clove of crushed
garlic and 1 small teaspoon
of golden sesame seeds to the dressing.
It will keep for 4–5 days in a
jar in the refrigerator.

PEANUT & GINGER DRESSING

Preparation: 5 minutes

For 2 or 3 bowls

50 g (2 oz) unsweetened peanut butter
juice of 1 small lemon
4 tablespoons sweet soy sauce
1 garlic clove, crushed
10 g (½ oz) fresh ginger root, peeled and grated
salt and pepper

method

Mix the peanut butter with
3–4 tablespoons of hot water.
Add all the other ingredients. Mix
together thoroughly. Taste and
adjust the seasoning if necessary.
You can also add a little chopped
chilli to the dressing.
It will keep for 3–4 days in a
jar in the refrigerator.
If it turns solid, dilute with
a little hot water.

GOCHUJANG DRESSING

Preparation: 5 minutes

For 2 or 3 bowls

1 tablespoon gochujang (Korean chilli paste)
2 tablespoons sweet soy sauce
2 tablespoons rice vinegar
½ teaspoon sesame seeds, toasted

method

Mix the gochujang with 2 tablespoons
of hot water. Add the rest of the
ingredients. The dressing will
keep for 4–5 days in a jar
in the refrigerator.

CREAMY VEGAN DRESSING

Preparation: 5 minutes

For 2 or 3 bowls

200 g (7 oz) silken tofu
1 garlic clove
1 small tablespoon wholegrain mustard
1 heaped tablespoon nutritional yeast flakes
1 squeeze of lemon juice
2 tablespoons olive oil
salt and pepper

method

Blend all the ingredients with a hand-held blender. Season to taste. Should be eaten quickly. The dressing will keep for 1 day in the refrigerator.

YOGHURT & HERB DRESSING

Preparation: 5 minutes

For 2 or 3 bowls

100 g (3½ oz) Greek yoghurt
20 g (¾ oz) fresh herbs, leaves picked: flat-leaf parsley, chives,
    mint, dill, chervil, etc.
1 small garlic clove
1 squeeze of lemon juice
2 tablespoons olive oil
salt and pepper

method

Blitz all the ingredients in a blender or with a hand-held blender. Season to taste
and add the lemon juice. Taste and adjust the seasoning if necessary.
For a vegan version, replace the yoghurt with silken tofu and
add 1 tablespoon of nutritional yeast.

SAVOURY GRANOLA

Preparation: 5 minutes
Cooking time: 25 minutes

For 1 jar

1 egg white
1 tablespoon maple syrup
1 tablespoon garlic powder
4 tablespoons olive oil
½ teaspoon salt
1 level teaspoon ground pepper

100 g (3½ oz/1 cup) rolled oats
80 g (2¾ oz/scant ⅔ cup) pecans, roughly chopped
70 g (2¼ oz/⅔ cup) pumpkin seeds
35 g (1¼ oz/scant ¼ cup) flaxseeds
35 g (1¼ oz/generous ¼ cup) sunflower seeds
30 g (1 oz/scant ¼ cup) sesame seeds

method

Preheat a fan oven to 180°C (400°F/gas 6). In a mixing bowl, whisk the egg white with the maple syrup, garlic powder, oil, salt and pepper. Add all the other ingredients. Mix well and spread on a baking tray. Bake for 25 minutes, stirring occasionally. The granola is ready when dry and golden brown. Allow to cool before storing in a jar. It will keep for several months in a dry place.

SPICED CHICKPEAS

Preparation: 5 minutes
Cooking time: 25 or 40 minutes

Serves 4

240 g (8½ oz) tinned chickpeas (garbanzos), drained
1 tablespoon ground cumin
1 tablespoon paprika

1 teaspoon ground pepper
½ teaspoon salt
4 tablespoons olive oil

method

Preheat the oven to 200°C fan (425°F/gas 7). Pat the chickpeas dry with some paper towel. Combine all the ingredients in a mixing bowl. Pour onto a baking tray. Lower the temperature to 170°C (375°F/gas 3). Bake for 25 minutes for chickpeas that are still soft and should be eaten within two days, or bake for 40 minutes for golden and crunchy chickpeas that will keep for 1 week in a jar.

VEGETABLE PATTIES

Preparation: 10 minutes
Cooking time: 15 minutes

Serves 2 (8 patties)

65 g (2¼ oz/generous ½ cup) flour
1 tablespoon cornflour (cornstarch)
    + 1 teaspoon baking powder
130 g (4½ oz) vegetables, grated or finely sliced:
    carrot, courgette (zucchini), cabbage, Chinese
    (napa) cabbage, kohlrabi, onion,
    sweet potato, pumpkin, potato,

(bell) pepper, parsnip, kimchi, etc.
1 garlic clove, crushed
120 ml (4 fl oz/½ cup) water
1 small teaspoon salt
5 tablespoons vegetable oil
pepper

method

Combine all the ingredients in a mixing bowl. Season with pepper. Heat the oil in a large frying pan (skillet). Add small piles of mixture to the pan and cook for 3–4 minutes on each side. The patties should be golden brown. You can also add sesame seeds or a spice (curry, turmeric, ginger, etc.) to the batter.

DHAL

Preparation: 10 minutes
Cooking time: 15 minutes

Serves 2 to 4

2 tablespoons olive oil
1 small onion, finely chopped
1 tablespoon garam masala
125 g (4½ oz/½ cup) red lentils
1 large tomato, cut into pieces

250 ml (8 fl oz/1 cup) coconut milk
80 ml (2½ fl oz/5 tablespoons) water
½ bunch of coriander (cilantro), chopped
salt

method

Heat the oil in a saucepan and sweat the onion for 3 minutes.
Add the garam masala, lentils, tomato, coconut milk
and water. Cover and cook over a low heat for 12 minutes. Stir regularly.
Add half a teaspoon of salt. Check the seasoning and continue cooking,
adding a little water if necessary. Remove from
the heat and add the coriander.

INDIAN RICE

Preparation: 10 minutes
Cooking time: 40 minutes

For about 4 bowls

200 g (7 oz/1 cup) long-grain brown rice + twice its
    volume of vegetable stock
2 tablespoons coconut oil
1 onion, finely chopped
1 garlic clove, crushed
40 g (1½ oz) fresh ginger root, peeled and grated

40 g (1½ oz/⅓ cup) raisins1 bay leaf
1 cinnamon stick
6 cloves
1 tablespoon turmeric

method

Rinse the rice. Heat the coconut oil in a sauté pan or saucepan. Sweat the onion, garlic and rice for 5 minutes. Add the stock and all the other ingredients. Bring to the boil. Lower the heat, cover and simmer for about 25 minutes. Reduce the heat to its lowest setting and continue cooking for another 10 minutes. Allow to stand for 5 minutes before mixing together and serving.

INDEX

Quadrille, Penguin Random House UK, One Embassy Gardens, 8 Viaduct Gardens, London SW11 7BW

Quadrille Publishing Limited is part of the Penguin Random House group of companies whose addresses can be found at global.penguinrandomhouse.com

First published in 2022 by Hachette Livre (Marabout), 2022. Original title: Bowls Veggie (ISBN 978-2-501-17083-3). This English Language edition published by Quadrille in 2024.

www.penguin.co.uk

A CIP catalogue record for this book is available from the British Library

ISBN 978-1-78488-700-1
10 9 8 7 6 5 4 3

FOR MARABOUT
Proofreader: Aurélie Legay and Véronique Dussidour
Design: Frederic Voisin

FOR QUADRILLE
Publishing Director: Kajal Mistry
Commissioning Editor: Kate Burkett
Senior Editor: Chelsea Edwards
Proofreader: Caroline West
Translator: Alison Murray
Typesetter: David Meikle
Senior Production Controller: Katie Jarvis

Colour reproduction by p2d
Printed in China by RR Donnelley Asia Printing Solutions Limited

The authorised representative in the EEA is Penguin Random House Ireland, Morrison Chambers, 32 Nassau Street, Dublin D02 YH68.

P enguin Random House is committed to a sustainable future for our business, our readers and our planet. This book is made from Forest Stewardship Council® certified paper.